PLATFORM PAPERS

QUARTERLY ESSAYS ON THE PERFORMING ARTS

No. 30
January 2012

CURRENCY HOUSE

The book has been printed on paper certified by the Programme for the Endorsement of Forest Certification (PEFC). PEFC is committed to sustainable forest management through third party forest certification of responsibly managed forests.

Indig-curious

Who can play Aboriginal roles?

JANE HARRISON

PLATFORM PAPERS

Quarterly essays from Currency House Inc.

Editor: Dr John Golder, j.golder@unsw.edu.au

Currency House Inc. is a non-profit association and resource centre advocating the role of the performing arts in public life by research, debate and publication.

Postal address: PO Box 2270, Strawberry Hills, NSW 2012, Australia

Email: info@currencyhouse.org.au Tel: (02) 9319 4953

Website: www.currencyhouse.org.au Fax: (02) 9319 3649

ISBN 978 0 9807982 9 6

ISSN 1449-583X

Typeset in 10.5 Arrus BT

Printed by Ligare Book Printers, Riverwood, NSW

Photo of Jane Harrison by Tatiana Doroshenko.

This edition of Platform Papers is supported by the Sidney Myer Fund, Neil Armfield, David Marr, Joanna Murray-Smith, Martin Portus, Alan Seymour and other individual donors and advisers. To them and to all our supporters Currency House extends sincere gratitude.

SIDNEY MYER FUND

Contents

AVAILABILITY *Platform Papers*, quarterly essays on the performing arts, is published every January, April, July and October and is available through bookshops or by subscription. Subscriptions or single copies can also be purchased on line in hard copy or electronic version from our website at www.currencyhouse.org.au

LETTERS Currency House invites reader to submit responses of 400–1000 words to the views expressed in this paper. To be published in the April issue they must be received by 15 February. Letters should be emailed to the Editor at info@currencyhouse.org.au

*I wish to dedicate this essay to my mother,
Shirley Angus.*

'Art through, during and from adversity'

The author

Jane Harrison is a descendant of the Muruwari people of NSW and combines work in the Aboriginal community sector with her writing activities. Since its première at the Melbourne International Festival, *Stolen*, her first play (1998), has been performed in Sydney, Adelaide, Tasmania, WA, the UK (twice), Hong Kong and Tokyo; has had readings in Canada and New York, and been performed most recently in Brisbane (2011). *Stolen* was the co-winner of the Kate Challis RAKA Award (2002) and has appeared on the English syllabi in Victoria and NSW. *Rainbow's End* premiered in Melbourne (2005), had a Tokyo production (2007), a season at Parramatta (2009), toured to 33 venues throughout eastern Australia in 2011 and is on the NSW English syllabus for 2009–12. *Blakvelvet* and *Custody* won the Inscriptions Indigenous Playwriting Prize (2006) and the Peter Holmes à Court Indigenous Playwriting Prize (2007) respectively. Jane co-wrote one episode of the SBS series *The Circuit* (2007). She contributed a chapter to *Many Voices, Reflections on Experiences of Indigenous Child Separation*, (National Library of Australia 2002); Her other essays include *My Journey through Stolen*, published in *Just Words?: Australian Authors on Writing and Justice* (University of Queensland Press 2008) and *Healing our Communities, Healing Ourselves* (2010) which won the *Medical Journal of Australia* Ross Ingram award. She convened the 2010 Victorian Premier's Literary Awards for Indigenous Writing and has an MA in Playwriting from QUT. She has two daughters.

Acknowledgements

Theatre is a collaborative animal, thankfully, especially Indigenous theatre, so I wish, first, to warmly thank all of the various cast members, directors, crew and theatre companies over the years for their courage, skills and conviction in bringing my plays to life. Thanks, too, to audiences for being willing to travel that journey with us. For help with this Platform Paper, I wish to thank a number of thoughtful, passionate and talented theatre practitioners who, through my interviews and conversations with them, contributed their voices, including Wesley Enoch, Rachael Maza, Leah Purcell and Sam Cook. Thanks also to Katharine Brisbane, Director of Currency House, and John Golder, Principal Editor, for the opportunity to be published and for their judicious comments and editing. This Platform Paper was based on my MA in Playwriting from Queensland University of Technology and I wish to thank my primary supervisor, David Megarrity. Finally, I wish to thank my two daughters, who are patient and supportive, particularly when deadlines are looming.

Introduction

Back in the 1920s Aboriginal writer David Unaipon was a committed collector of Aboriginal* stories and myths, which he shared with non-Aboriginal writers, urging them to 'use' them.[1] Was it his belief that non-Aboriginal writers should be free to utilize Aboriginal myths and stories without qualms, without recourse, without *responsibility*? Or did he merely hope that Aboriginal myths would be afforded the status and respect of the equivalent mythology hailing from Europe, that they would be valued as part of our country's cultural expression?

Unaipon can hardly have imagined that ninety years later two Russian ice dancers, competing in the European championships, would trip the ice fantastic, resplendent in brown 'painted up' body suits, faux eucalypt leaves and red loin cloths, to the throb of the didgeridoo. But world champions Oksana Domnina and Maxim Shabalin did just that, choosing for one routine an Aboriginal-themed 'folk' dance. It was a gesture that provoked considerable controversy. Aboriginal leaders were dismayed, calling the routine 'offensive', 'cultural theft' and citing it as a further example of the way Aboriginal culture was

* For ease of reading, the word 'Aboriginal' has been used interchangeably with Indigenous, to signify both Aboriginal and Torres Strait Islander peoples. I apologize if that offends.

'disrespected'. In a bid to have the routine banned, the NSW Land Council even took their concerns to the Australian Olympic Federation. Sol Bellear, of the NSW Aboriginal Land Council, said, 'We see it as stealing Aboriginal culture, and it is yet another example of the Aboriginal people of Australia being exploited.'[2] The reaction of one blogger was less heated:

> Perhaps Domnina and Shabalin have stepped on the thin ice the moment they decided to put together the program not of their own culture. Culture allows only authenticity. The indigenous Australians are trying to protect their rich and diverse cultural heritage. It takes more than research to accurately portray the 60,000-year-old culture. Also, the sports competition is by no means the right venue.[3]

It was reported that the dancers had researched the routine via the internet and had consulted no Aboriginal people regarding movements, music or costume. The routine ended with the couple rubbing noses, a traditional gesture of our neighbours, the Maori of New Zealand. While the Russians seemed at a loss to understand why their presentation had given offence, US champions Ben Agosto and Tanith Belbin, although no more culturally sensitive, tried to be more forgiving. 'We are all trying to portray a style of dance we aren't familiar with', said Agosto, to which his partner added:

> I know Oksana and Max as people, and I can assume they never intended to offend anyone with their program. They were just trying to create something unique and different, and they certainly achieved that. Hopefully [...] it all will work out.[4]

But, things didn't work out. For the routine's next outing, at the Vancouver Winter Olympics, the dancers ditched the brown face, but altered little else. The response was lukewarm, and they finished in third place.

Did expatriate, non-Aboriginal Australian Germaine Greer have in mind a similar use for Aboriginal themes when, in her Quarterly Essay *Whitefella Jump Up*, she declared that '[w]e can dance too'?[5] Did she mean that Aboriginal myths, stories and ceremonies also belong to non-Aboriginal people? When writing that '[f]or 200 years the Aboriginal peoples ha[d] been seducing the whitefellas, subtly drawing them into their web of dreams', was she implying that non-Aboriginal people could learn to integrate Aboriginality into their being?[6] Contrast the reaction to the Russian figure skaters with the rapturous reception given to the Chooky Dancers, a Yolgnu dance troupe who have re-interpreted 'Zorba the Greek' and turned it into a YouTube viral sensation—a reception that, significantly, has been especially positive on the part of the Greek community. Indeed, the troupe has been invited to perform their interpretation in Greece. Perhaps the difference between these two examples of cultural expression lies in the fact that the Chooky Dancers were not 'pretending' to be Greek: they didn't wear makeup to change their racial characteristics nor parody a Greek costume. They used Mikas Theodorakis's film score, and while this music has become synonymous with Greek culture—it is based on a traditional 'butcher's' dance—it was only written for the 1964 film, in which Anthony Quinn, a Mexican, starred as the Greek Zorba. Perhaps, as a more 'modern' variation on a traditional dance, it does not carry the same cultural weight as something intended to represent a traditional ceremonial Aboriginal dance?

So how do non-Aboriginal performance practitioners access Aboriginal themes? Can they? Should they? Is there a place for political correctness in performance? Since Aboriginal people are sensitive to the way their cultural motifs are used does that mean there is no opportunity for them to be integrated into non-Aboriginal cultural expression? Or, as in the case of the Russian skaters, is the condemnation an appropriate response to an offensive appropriation of Aboriginal culture?

1

The challenges: what causes offence?

Who is writing about us and why?

In literature, in particular, non-Aboriginal Australians are weaving Aboriginal themes and characters into their writing. Protocols, many developed by Aboriginal experts, guide the writer through this process. However, these protocols do not always translate to performance and performers. So what are the constraints upon the non-Aboriginal performer in relation to Aboriginal themes? Some argue that it is the actor's role to use their skill to portray a character, regardless of their race, gender or age. If this is the case, can they 'learn' to portray an Aboriginal character on stage? Can it ever be acceptable for a non-Aboriginal actor to perform an Aboriginal role—and who should decide, the white audience, or the Aboriginal audience? Do these two audiences have the same expectations of what is presented on stage? What are the barriers faced by non-Aboriginal performers in playing Aboriginal roles and how might Aboriginal themes be incorporated into mainstream productions? How, if ever, can Aboriginal themes be 'used' in a way that is acceptable to Aboriginal people? Neither Sophocles nor Shakespeare is around to praise or to shudder at the way in which their work is interpreted today, but Aboriginal people are alive and well and are outspoken about the way in which they are depicted on the page, stage and on the screen.

I began to muse on these issues when I, a playwright with Aboriginal heritage (Muruwari) who writes Aboriginal-themed plays (*Stolen*, *Rainbow's End*, *Blakvelvet*, for example), was commissioned to write a play based on 'Indigenous themes' for two non-Aboriginal actor/producers. I pondered how to write an 'Indigenous-themed' play for non-Indigenous performers, wondering what I could get away with, and what I could not. (It is important to note that the commissioning actors had no intention of playing Aboriginal characters.) As a playwright I am interested in pushing the boundaries and inciting audiences to think. My intention, however, is always to produce work that is respectful of Aboriginal audiences, whom I consider to be my primary audience, and I have no wish to antagonize the Aboriginal community by creating work that is offensive or divisive.

Little has been written on how the non-Aboriginal performer accesses Aboriginal themes. This may be explained by the small body of Aboriginal plays, the relatively few Aboriginal playwrights, and the resulting smaller pool of critical thinking that relates specifically to Aboriginal theatre. Indeed, the Aboriginal playwright is a relatively recent phenomenon: Kevin Gilbert can claim to be the first performed Aboriginal playwright with his play *The Cherry Pickers* (1968). It was not until 1978 that Currency Press published *The Cake Man*, by Aboriginal writer Robert Merritt. Since so little has been written about Aboriginal theatre, I have drawn upon exemplars from literature, film, television and art, dance and music that incorporate Aboriginal themes, examining works that have been created by Aboriginal and non-Aboriginal artists both locally, in Australia, and also internationally, particularly from colonized countries, where Indigenous populations are grappling with similar issues of appropriation and cultural expression.

I have coined the term 'Indig-curious'—with a nod to the term 'bi-curious'—to signify those who are curious about Aboriginal culture and people, especially when, as non-Aboriginal, they are coming from a low knowledge base, but have a passion to understand more.

****

One trend that has emerged in recent years is for non-Aboriginal Australian fiction writers to incorporate Aboriginal themes or to write Aboriginal characters into their narratives. In fiction, Alex Miller's *Journey to the Stone Country* (2002) and Kate Grenville's *The*

Secret River (2005) are award-winning examples. More specifically in theatre, since the late 1920s there have been a number of plays, by non-Aboriginal writers, with Aboriginal characters: Katharine Susannah Prichard's *Brumby Innes* (1927), for example, Dorothy Hewett's *The Man from Mukinupin* (1979) and Thomas Keneally's *Bullie's House* (1981). It is not my intention here to critique the content of these plays, nor to analyse how the authors went about researching the Aboriginality of the characters or themes. I simply note that these non-Aboriginal playwrights had the self-belief to write their plays. Similarly, the theatre companies concerned had the confidence to present them. In the 'General Feedback on Entries' submitted for the 2006 short play festival, *Short + Sweet*, the judges drew attention to the influx of scripts dealing with 'white guilt' (their term): over twenty plays dealt with on issues of reconciliation and relationships between Aboriginal and non-Aboriginal Australians.[7]

Why do non-Aboriginal playwrights feel the need to write Aboriginal characters/stories? How can they feel confident they can write these characters sensitively, giving them authentic voices? How do they research their material? How do they ensure—indeed, do they feel the need to ensure—that the Aboriginal community is happy with their work? Aboriginal film director Rachel Perkins suggests that in order to write Aboriginal characters a non-Aboriginal author must take a multi-faceted approach, as Louis Nowra did in the screenplay of *Radiance* (1998), which she directed:

> [Nowra] had done his research, he's lived it, his coming from a position of being very informed and when you've got those things, ability, talent,

> research, and experience, you can write or create on any level, regardless of your race.[8]

Not everyone feels as inclusive as Perkins. Aboriginal academic Anita Heiss argues:

> The 1990s saw increased discussion, both within and outside the Indigenous community, on the issue of non-Indigenous writers writing about Aboriginal society and culture. For some non-Indigenous writers working in the area, their case for doing so gains credibility as they are seen to be providing a voice (however indirectly) to Aboriginal Australia. However, this attitude is unacceptable to many Indigenous writers who are tired of competing with white writers for the opportunity to write and be published in the area that is particularly and specifically related to their lives.[9]

Today Aboriginal writers have the opportunity to present their own stories; publishers are more willing to publish them; theatres—including mainstream—are prepared to program them, and audiences eager to read or see them. This is not a long-standing phenomenon, and the creative output is far from massive. Indeed, until 1968 and Gilbert's *The Cherry Pickers*, Aboriginal characters in plays were the constructs of non-Aboriginal authors, or, as Sonja Kurtzer writes, 'It has been the oppressor who has sought to define Aboriginality'.[10] It is the inaccuracy of their portrayals that is in part responsible for our dissatisfaction with non-Aboriginal writers telling 'our stories for us'. 'I do not like the way [...] our histories have been smudged, distorted and hidden, or written for us', says Alexis Wright:

> I want our people to have books, their own books, in their own communities, and written by our own people. I want the truth to be told, our truths, so, first and foremost, I hold my pen for the suffering in our communities.[11]

Rachael Maza, Aboriginal actor and Artistic Director of Ilbijerri Theatre Cooperative, makes the point unequivocally:

> We've had a history of being mis-represented, so now we have more power to address the balance. It is about understanding when there is an Indigenous story, and if there is not the Indigenous person to tell it, then don't do it.

So when a non-Aboriginal author writes an Aboriginal character, or when a dancer, fine artist or musician references, mimics or is 'influenced by' Aboriginal culture, is it considered cultural appropriation, or is it a desirable movement, a natural extension of the curiosity non-Aboriginal people might have about a unique, rich culture than has for so long been invisible or ignored?

We need to ask why non-Aboriginal writers and arts practitioners feel the need to incorporate Aboriginal themes at all. While Alex Miller's *Journey to the Stone Country* and Kate Grenville's *The Secret River* both received critical acclaim for their sensitive treatment of Aboriginal themes and characters, they were the work of novelists who boldly went, as Andrea Stretton put it, 'where angels dare not tread'.[12] Peter Pierce adds:

> Miller also accepts the challenge to write of Aboriginal people. It is thirty years since Thomas Keneally did so in *The Chant of Jimmie Blacksmith*.

> Since then Keneally has reflected that he must have been 'a fucking madman' to undertake such a venture.[13]

As more non-Aboriginal writers interact with Aboriginal people, in the way that Miller does—his Aboriginal character, Bo Rennie, is modeled on a real-life friend—do they earn the right to create from an Aboriginal perspective? Have we reached a point in our country's creative journey where these themes are so 'fashionable' that writing about them is almost *de rigueur*, as novelist Carmel Bird suggested in 2001, when commenting on the launch of a colleague's novel about a crime:

> There were no Aboriginal characters in the story, and no Aboriginal issues or questions either. Yet a woman in the crowd made the comment that the author had not, in this novel, dealt with the current Aboriginal issues. It was a very strange comment [...], which, just a few years ago, would have been virtually impossible to frame. The idea that a reader would now have an expectation that a contemporary Australian novel absolutely must display some attitude to matters of Aboriginality is a very twenty-first-century idea.

Bird, who has herself written about the Stolen Generations, goes on to answer her own rhetorical question:

> In a sense the woman who commented on the absence of Aboriginal issues in a work of current fiction was right on track, and it has become—I say this as a writer of fiction—difficult not to include the issue of race in the writing of fiction, because

> the questions are so urgent and so current, so perpetually present in one's heart.[14]

Theatre director Wesley Enoch points out that some non-Aboriginal people are writing stories that tell 'white' history/stories, but include interactions with Aboriginal characters. This, he says, is a natural and pertinent part of our shared history. He uses the example of Andrew Bovell, who in *Holy Day* was not attempting to write an 'Aboriginal' play, but acknowledging the role Aboriginal people have played in white lives and narratives. But beyond the why, there is 'how' Aboriginal people are portrayed, and this is more problematic.

How one is represented, whether on a book, stage or screen, is important for Aboriginal people and has a political imperative, according to Aboriginal academic Marcia Langton, who writes: '[T]o demand complete control of all representation [...] is to demand censorship, to deny the communication which none of us can prevent'.[15] She quotes E. Ann Kaplan, who advocates, as an alternative, a 'decentering of Western culture' via a 'dialogue with the other culture [...] within frameworks we bring with us'.[16]

A major part of the criticism is driven by a desire on the part of the audience for an 'authentic' discourse. This audience is often non-Aboriginal, and this is somewhat ironic, as the Aboriginal writer's principal aim is to create images and stories for their own community; entertaining the non-Aboriginal audience is secondary. Yet they are an audience, and cannot be ignored, and they have expectations of the genre. Sonja Kurtzer postulates that 'Aboriginal literature meets the desires of the hegemonic culture to hear "authentic" tales of the "other"'. She goes on to state that at a 1996 conference for Indigenous writers and playwrights delegates noted that:

> When they speak, they do more than just tell about their lives as individuals. Their stories are seen to represent a body of knowledge [...] As autobiographical texts, the stories are seen to represent the truth. Therefore issues of cultural maintenance and integrity are extremely important to the indigenous community.[17]

The 2010 Big hART/Belvoir production of *Namatjira* illustrated this point. As I sat watching a community-night performance, I felt that neither I nor the other Aboriginal people in attendance were the intended audience. Maybe we weren't. For me, and a few Aboriginal colleagues who also saw the production, it had the disconcerting air of sometimes slipping into 'white'. In Wesley Enoch's words:

> While [*Namatjira*] is fantastic, there are some moments when the writer Scott Rankin appears in the mouth of the character. The character's Aboriginality is not from the inside but seen from the outside.

That might have been for purely pragmatic reasons, for like the work of Aboriginal artists that hangs on white walls, Aboriginal theatre does not have the numbers to provide a large, paying audience. (Most major productions have a free or low-cost community night to make work with Aboriginal content accessible to Aboriginal audiences.) Theatre critic Alison Croggon goes further than Enoch, and says that 'the 'show [is] consciously directed towards a white audience. White attitudes to Aboriginality are gently mocked, but this is never alienating; instead, mischievously, it invites its audience into its world.'[18] This is despite Rankin's strong engagement with the community about (and with) whom he was writing. Enoch asks, 'How do you get inside the clan?' It is a rhetorical question. Furthermore, if it's so hard for a writer to get 'inside the clan', is it any easier for a performer?

Perhaps the growing trend for non-Aboriginal writers to tackle Aboriginal themes or to write Aboriginal characters is aided by the existence of protocol documents, developed in consultation with Indigenous people, such as those produced by the Australia Council for the Arts?[19] Of course, protocol documents can only provide guidelines; not following them may prevent a writer from receiving funding from entities such as the Australia Council, but the guidelines themselves cannot prevent people from writing about Aboriginal themes inaccurately (as Marlo Morgan did in his 1990 *Mutant Message Down Under*) or critically (as Louis Nowra did in *Bad Dreaming* in 2007).[20]

So in many ways this strand of the debate is moot; many non-Aboriginal writers and playwrights are already writing Aboriginal characters: the horse has bolted. For performers, the territory is still contested.

2

Aboriginal themes, can they be defined?

Wherever Aboriginal peoples co-exist with colonizing peoples the question is asked, 'What are Aboriginal themes?' But first we need to ask: 'Who is 'Aboriginal?'. The accepted definition is straightforward: a person is Aboriginal if they meet three criteria: have Aboriginal heritage, identify as Aboriginal and are accepted within the community as Aboriginal.[21]

While establishing descent can be challenging for some, for me it is the third of these criteria that presents most challenges, as 'acceptance' is out of the individual's control, and depends on who is doing the 'accepting' or 'rejecting'. For example, some members of the community might accept a person, while others might reject them, for complex reasons. Often people are categorized—by others, often non-Aboriginal others—by their looks, especially their skin colour. But identity is far more complex than that. As a light-skinned person of Aboriginal heritage, I find that non-Aboriginal people are more likely to question my Aboriginality than Aboriginal people. At one public-speaking event an audience member declared that I 'didn't look Aboriginal, didn't sound Aboriginal and didn't dress like an Aboriginal. I was so well dressed.'[22] However, defining Aboriginality can be problematic, both within and outside the Aboriginal community. As Marcia Langton has observed, there is a problem in 'indeterminacy' of categories such as 'Aboriginal', 'race' and 'gender'.[23] And Carol Laseur's poststructuralist viewpoint is that 'Aboriginality is everywhere and nowhere simultaneously'.[24]

If defining who 'is' an Aboriginal presents challenges, then defining Aboriginal 'themes' or 'content' presents rather more. Are Aboriginal stories simply those that involve Aboriginal people/characters? Are they only traditional or Dreamtime stories? Are Aboriginal stories those that are controlled by Aboriginal creators, irrespective of the content? Or are there other considerations to be taken into account? Has the readership or audience anything to do with it?

In an essay on the work of Aboriginal filmmaker Traccy Moffat, Marcia Langton asks:

> Yet the question of what we perceive in watching these 'Indigenous' film and video oeuvres is as puzzling as Aboriginal identity itself. Does the content become 'Aboriginal' by handing the camera over to the Aboriginal person?[25]

In theatre, there is a clear set of themes that are recognizably 'Aboriginal'—or at least that's what the 'Teacher's Notes' for *Page 8*, David Page's autobiographical one-man play seems to believe:

> Provide your students with a copy of the Contemporary Aboriginal Theatre table. Ask them to create their own table for *Page 8*, using three columns to identify the features of the performance that correspond to the features of contemporary aboriginal [*sic*] theatre.[26]

Contemporary Aboriginal Theatre Related Study Areas

Dramatic Form

Non-Linear Narrative	Eclectic and Fragmented

A combination of the styles and traditions of Western performance with aspects of Indigenous language and culture

Thematic Concerns

Grief	Kinship/Family Relationships
Identity	Assimilation
The Stolen Generation	Racism
Reconciliation	Connection with the land
Interactions with the law	Effects of the past on the present

Dramatic Techniques and Conventions

Direct Audience Address	Symbolism
Visual Metaphor	Dance and Music
Storytelling	Multi Media
Indigenous Language	Political Oratory
Presentational Acting	Realism
Stand up comedy	

Matthew Clausen, *Page 8: Teacher's Notes*, Sydney Opera House.

While some themes ('grief', 'identity' etc.) are commonplace in non-Aboriginal plays, others— 'Stolen Generation' and 'connection with the land', in particular—are strongly associated with the Aboriginal play. But do they *define* the 'Aboriginal play'? Is the 'Aboriginal play' *obliged* to deal with one or more of those themes? Three Aboriginal playwrights of my acquaintance have told me that they have submitted proposals to theatre companies based on their own lives. All were rejected, with the suggestion that the stories were not 'Aboriginal enough'. In each case, their stories told of a personal journey as urban Aboriginal people, and were not concerned with political ideas or the 'larger' issues faced by Aboriginal people. I would argue that they are Aboriginal plays, as they tell stories of lives led by individuals who identify as Aboriginal and have lived lives defined by their Aboriginality.

To analyze the elements of an Aboriginal play, it is useful to look at a range of plays by Aboriginal writers, grouping them by thematic concerns. There are autobiographical plays, which tend to be characterized by tales of hardship and survival and leavened by humour; these include Jimmy Chi's *Bran Nue Dae* (1991), Ningali Lawford's *Ningali* (1994), Leah Purcell's *Box the Pony* (1997), Deborah Cheetham's *White Baptist Abba Fan* (1997), Tammy Anderson's *I Don't Wanna Play House* (2001) and David Page's *Page 8* (2004). In the view of Maryrose Casey, some of these, monodramas by female playwrights, have been used

> as a powerful form of talking back. [...] *Ningali* (1994), *7 Stages of Grieving* (1994) and *Box the Pony* (1997), [...] created by Indigenous women, often in collaboration with others, explored their personal biographies as a way of revealing the broader social and political framework.[27]

There are also a number of biographical plays: *Aliwa!* (2000) is based on the lives of Aboriginal playwright Jack Davis's sisters, while Tony Briggs's *The Sapphires* (2004) centres on the experiences of his mother and aunties. There are some, but still only a few, with purely fictional storylines, including John Harding's *Enuff* (2002), Mitch Torres's *One Day in '67* (2002) and Wesley Enoch's *Black Medea* (2000) which reframes the Greek tragedy, adding layers of domestic violence and cultural desecration. My own play *Rainbow's End* (2005) has fictional characters, but incorporates real places and events from the 1950s.

Sonja Kurtzer has argued that the audience for the Aboriginal writers' product is 'constrained by a need to present in a way that a white audience sees as valid, yet unthreatening'. Therefore, '[w]hen Aboriginal people contribute to the discourse on Aboriginality they do not do so from a "free" space'.[28] One ubiquitous motif is the image of the downtrodden. Political themes also abound. For example, as Katharine Brisbane observes, Jack Davis's plays deal regularly with 'job discrimination, land rights and the high incidence of black deaths in custody' as well as the removal of children and assimilation.[29]

When it comes to the non-Aboriginal writer, the mythical, spiritual Aboriginal character seems to be an attractive exemplar, particularly in film. S/he is mystical, earthy, wise, often uneducated, natural, has a profound relationship with the land, is spiritual, mysterious, esoteric, unfashionable, innocent, non-consumerist, working-class, family-oriented and fringe-dwelling. Nullah, the young Aboriginal boy in Baz Luhrmann's film *Australia* (2008) perfectly illustrates this archetype, as do many of the roles played by David Gulpilil.

In a previous role as artistic coordinator at Ilbijerri Theatre Cooperative I sometimes received requests from non-Aboriginal filmmakers looking for an actor to play an Aboriginal character. Inevitably, the character, written by earnest young scriptwriters, would display some 'mystical' dimension that is at odds with our largely secular society, yet acceptable to an Australian audience in the way that it would not be if given to a 'white' character. A religious white character—I acknowledge that 'mystical' and 'religious' are not synonymous, of course—might easily be a target for derision. Perhaps the spiritual Aboriginal is an extension of the 'noble savage' construct, whereby traditional Aboriginal people are more 'noble', more 'inherently good', and non-Aboriginals are civilized and hence degenerate? I am not implying that Aboriginal people are not spiritual, but that for non-Aboriginal people on the 'outside', their viewpoint of Aboriginal spirituality may be idealized, rather than grounded in reality.

Is it these 'romantic' qualities that attract the non-Aboriginal writer to develop an Aboriginal character? Does this romanticizing of Aboriginal characters distract from the development of other kinds of story that might reflect the diversity and increasing urbanization of Aboriginal people, causing the 'authentic' stories of an urbanized group to be viewed as 'inauthentic' by the dominant white society?

If drama is about conflict then the Aboriginal story will be intrinsically more dramatic. There is a harsh context to our lives: social indicators show that Aboriginal people have a life expectancy 15–20 years lower than that of other Australians, a lower employment rate and higher custody rate, and are far more likely to die in custody.[30] Only 33% of Indigenous Australians finish school, compared to the national average of 77% and only 30% of Aboriginal families own their own home compared to 70% of other Australians.[31] These social determinants only hint at the tragedy and layers of intergenerational trauma that play out in Aboriginal lives on a daily basis. So perhaps the tragedy inherent in many Aboriginal lives provides a unique and ready-made storyline for theatrical exploration that may be in contrast to the paucity of 'drama' in the majority of white, middle-class lives, most of which has been mined by David Williamson. More generously, perhaps non-Aboriginal Australians are finally recognizing our shared history, and that, as Carmel Bird noted, the Aboriginal voice can no longer be ignored.

3

Why are they writing (and painting) like us?

'Aboriginal culture' is another amorphous term, one that can be meaningless by trying to be all-encompassing. It is argued that there is no one 'Aboriginal culture'.

There were more than 500 dialects before white contact and a vast array of cultural practices, so trying to put them all into one neat package is impossibly reductive. 'Aboriginality' can be reduced to a set of symbols: 'traditional', northern Australian motifs equal Aboriginal culture. Painted up (dark) skins, ochre colours, red, black and yellow together, the Aboriginal flag (originally designed as a flag for land rights, but now embraced as the Aboriginal flag) dot paintings or raark (cross-hatching), boomerangs, didgeridoos and clap sticks, all coalesce into an instantly recognizable aesthetic. However, for the urban Aboriginal these traditional elements can be almost as foreign, inappropriate, artificial or even superficial as they are to some non-Aboriginal people. Many (particularly those removed from their families and communities) have elements of traditional culture, such as ceremonies and language, that have been lost, stolen or deprived of meaning. This is not to suggest that there is no urban, or south-eastern, Aboriginal culture, simply that it's not *synonymous* with traditional culture. Our culture, for us, is an evolving thing, just as theirs is for non-Aboriginal people.

****

As Aboriginal cultural output has developed a following, it has become a commodity with enormous monetary value. Think of the prices paid for the work of artists such as Rover Thomas, Emily Kame Kngwarreye and Clifford Possum Tjapaltjarri. Aboriginal artist Richard Bell has declared Aboriginal art to be 'a white thing', and criticizes the too-dominant role that non-Aborigines play in the management or 'business' of his art form:

> Aboriginal Art has become a product of the times. [...] The result of a concerted and sustained marketing strategy, albeit one that has been loose and uncoordinated. There is no Aboriginal Art Industry. There is, however, an industry that caters for Aboriginal Art. The key players in that industry are not Aboriginal. They are mostly White people whose areas of expertise are in the fields of anthropology and 'Western Art' [...T]hose issues conspire to condemn it to non-Aboriginal control.[32]

Perhaps it is because Aboriginal creative outputs are different and counter-intuitively 'exotic' that Aboriginal culture has taken on the role of 'unique selling proposition', to employ the lingua franca of the marketing world. The marketing of the signs and symbols of Aboriginal Australia are visible everywhere, from the uniforms of Qantas stewards to the opening ceremony of the Sydney Olympic and Melbourne

Commonwealth Games. For Germaine Greer these symbols are our only identifiers:

> Australia's only way of branding itself in the world market has been to co-opt the insignia of Aboriginality, with didgeridoos, boomerangs, spot [*sic*] paintings and skeleton animal shapes.[33]

The commodification of Aboriginal culture has provided a breeding ground for exploitation, exemplified by a number of literary hoaxes in which authors have falsely identified themselves as Aboriginal. Serbian immigrant Sreten Bozic published *The Track to Bralgu* (1977) under the authorship of 'B. Wongar', a fabrication. Wanda Koolmatrie, ostensibly an Aboriginal woman, won a life-writing award for *My Own Sweet Time* (1994) before being exposed as Leon Carmen, a white male.[34] Rosemary van den Berg, an Elder of the Nyoongar people, who has rightly condemned 'these cheats who are stealing Aboriginal identities', believes Aboriginal people are now 'fightin' back' after years of exploitation.[35]

But what of performance modes where the lines have blurred—music, for example? White boys rap, Aboriginal girls rap, a musical style that began with African and Latino Americans. For some white Australian musicians, the years of collaboration with Aboriginal musicians have led to trust—or, more accurately, years of trust have led to collaboration. When the Aboriginal collective Black Arm Band gave their first concert, *murundak* ('alive' in Woiwurrung) at the 2006 Melbourne International Arts Festival, Shane Howard, a white colleague who played with them, declared:

> We've seen a new Australia and we're not going back. It's not black and white any more. People like myself and Neil (Murray) and Paul (Kelly) and Peter Garrett, so many whitefellas now have been out there, interacting with Aboriginal people, and we're beyond colour. We're brothers and sisters.[36]

Most people would agree that cultural appropriation is inappropriate. But what of that subtle variation, 'referencing', whereby one work is based on another? Aboriginal artist Gordon Bennett references other artists: Van Gogh, Jackson Pollock, Hans Heysen, Margaret Preston, Jean-Michel Basquiat. But who would dare criticize Bennett when *his* referencing is seen as an act of political defiance:

> Bennett's referencing, appropriation and recontextualisation of familiar images and art styles challenges conventional ways of viewing and thinking and opens up new possibilities for understanding the subjects Bennett explores.[37]

Imants Tillers, a non-Aboriginal artist, also has a long practice of referencing artists such as Van Gogh and also the Aboriginal artists Michael Jagamara Nelson and Emily Kame Kngwarreye. Like Carmel Bird he believes it is 'impossible today for an Australian artist not to take Aboriginal art into account, into serious consideration'.[38] Anthropologist Howard Morphy, who writes extensively about Aboriginal art, believes that by incorporating Michael Jagamara Nelson's *Five Dreamings* (1982) prominently into his own *The Nine Shots* (1985), Tillers

> opened himself up to accusations of appropriating Aboriginal imagery without permission and

> impinging on the moral rights of the artist. The offence was compounded by the very 'placedness' of Aboriginal art, its apparent inseparability from locality. Aboriginal art was in place and Tillers' art apparently challenged identities based on locality, removed images from their cultural contexts, and juxtaposed them with images from other places and times.

In return, Bennett borrowed imagery from Tillers for his *The Nine Ricochets* (1990). Tillers continued to incorporate Aboriginal symbols and themes after 1985, but always with 'permission [...] granted and collaboration acknowledged'. Indeed, he developed 'a personal relationship with Michael Jagamara Nelson, whose work he had originally incorporated into his own without permission'. If Tillers' work takes a postcolonial approach to Aboriginal art—i.e. belongs to a time when that art is acknowledged and accorded appropriate credit—'does that mean', Morphy asks provocatively, 'almost by definition that it [Tillers' art] has become more Aboriginal?' His conclusion, however, is that

> [w]hile 'borrowing from', 'being influenced by', 'finding inspiration in', 'learning from', and 'building upon' other people's artworks is always going to be an integral part of art practice, it is never going to be without its dangers.[39]

What implications are there in Morphy's proposition for theatre performance? If a non-Aboriginal actor 'inhabits' an Aboriginal character, does s/he *become* more Aboriginal? While actor Rachael Maza acknowledges that 'actors have always played roles beyond their own experiences', to me, 'Aboriginality' is about 'being', about 'the *lived experience*', not the artificial approximation on stage that has been gleaned by osmosis over a limited timespan.

A subtle variant of 'referencing' is 'mimicking', or 'closely imitating'. For example, in 2006 Australian Ballet dancers collaborated on *Rites*, a Bangarra Dance Theatre-devised show. *The Sun Herald* reviewer found it 'fascinating to watch Australian Ballet principal artist Steven Heathcote adopting indigenous moves'.[40] Is this what Greer had in mind, I wonder, in asserting that 'we can dance too'?

Bangarra's artistic director Stephen Page describes how this collaboration began:

> I got all the [Australian B]allet dancers to take their ballet shoes off and let their hair out and everyone sat in a circle and I got a ballet dancer and a Bangarra dancer to come to the centre of the circle and made the ballet dancer just mimic the Bangarra dancer. So it was all very quiet, it was sort of like a little contemporary ritual. Once they observed each other in a style it's actually a really good way for them to learn.[41]

Once again, though, it is important to note *who it is that controls* the cross-cultural process. If Aboriginal people have a say in what transpires, then the collaboration is likely to be favourable. If the Bangarra dancers had been dancing with the Australian Ballet in an Aboriginal-themed production under a non-Aboriginal director/choreographer, the outcome may have not been so easily accepted. As Wesley Enoch observes, it is a matter of informed choices:

> A non-Aboriginal director will make choices using other criteria. In regards to Stephen Page and the

> Australian Ballet, as long as he is not using sacred material it is okay for him to teach non-Aboriginal dancers the steps; he's the one making those informed decisions. It is not right when a [non-Aboriginal] director wants the audience to think that the performance is Indigenous […] It is a little bit empty when it is just mimicry.

It is clear that there is no across-the-board, standard, one-size-fits-all protocol for the utilization of Aboriginal themes in artistic endeavours.

While funding bodies such as the Australia Council and state arts bodies have firm protocols in place for dealing with Aboriginal content, and suggest that the creative should consult, they don't spell out *how* to consult. As a writer, you might want to use a Dreamtime story in your play—but from whom do you ask permission to use this story? You might not know who the custodian of that story is, or who has the 'authority' to grant you permission. You might speak to one person in the community, but another Elder insists they have custodianship. These issues may be exacerbated by conflict between different mobs in an area. Gaining permission, therefore, can present a set of formidable challenges for both the non-Aboriginal and, the Aboriginal. Consultation can take considerable time. For a community struggling with more pressing issues, a request to use a particular story might not be a high priority. If you are not known, you may not be trusted. And why then should you be granted permission? After all, you might represent the oppressor. To an Aboriginal person a 'story' might be more than a mere tale, it might have sacred significance. The community has no way of controlling what you do with it; protocols are not legal imperatives, merely guides.

Consultation can go belly-up if the wrong people are approached, or if the consultation is not sufficiently thorough to satisfy all parties. Like Phillip Gwynne's novel *Deadly, Unna?*, upon which it is based, Paul Goldman's 2002 film, *Australian Rules*, depicts real events, in particular a fatal shooting. This incident, or rather the admissibility of its being dealt with by a white author, divided the Aboriginal community of Point Pearce, where the actual events took place. Aboriginal broadcaster Kelrick Martin spells out the issues:

> Whether or not th[e] consultation [that took place between the Point Pearce community and the filmmakers] was adequate is definitely in question [...] And whoever granted permission on the community's behalf was not the true representative Elder of Point Pearce. He says one 'yes' does not qualify as permission. And you must clarify the correct person to speak on behalf of others.[42]

Consultation and collaboration take time and effort—and the results are not always satisfactory. 'Indig-curious' creatives are often confused about where to start, and let it fall into the too-hard basket.

Some believe the ownership of Aboriginal themes should rest in Aboriginal hands. As bicultural Canadian writer Kateri Akiwenzie-Damm puts it, '[W]riters need to write about what they know.

> When you try to write from some other perspective, you do so at your own peril. [...] I think it's easier for [Aboriginal writers] to write [from a non-Aboriginal perspective] because we've been forced

> into those school systems, we've been forced into mainstream society. We're fluent in the language. Many of us are forced to be bicultural. So it's not really being untrue because it's already part of who we are and part of our knowledge base [...] Readers consciously or subconsciously pick up on it when somebody is not truthful.

The frustrations of audiences, and the playwrights who write for them, regarding the glut of plays about the 'white middle-class experience' are not new. Writing about his 1985 New York production of Tom Keneally's *Bullie's House*, in which Aboriginal actors Justine Saunders and Ernie Dingo played the Aboriginal characters, director Kenneth Frankel noted:

> We felt we had to do a play like this, that said something different [...] I think theater here is becoming staid, five people sitting around waiting for the phone to ring or for a knock on the door. This play goes back to more theatricality, and we felt it was worth bringing actors all the way from Australia to do it.[44]

Cultural appropriation and control of images and themes are challenging issues that this essay can only skim. There is no doubt that non-Aboriginal people are fascinated and curious, wanting to draw upon the rich cultural traditions of Aboriginal Australia, and to express them through storytelling, dance, art, music or performance. But there is a strong feeling of exploitation when non-Aboriginal people 'use' Aboriginal cultural heritage as if it were their right to do so. I'm sure that is not what David Uniapon intended. Aboriginal people need to have control over the output, for cultural and business reasons, as well as reasons of authenticity, the latter being of great importance to both the Aboriginal audience and the non-Aboriginal audience.

4

Responsibility, anxiety and guilt: the burdens of the message maker

Aboriginal writers and actors carry a far greater weight of responsibility to their community than their white counterparts for the way in which they create their characters. The closest parallel might be that of the way they draw on the personal experiences of family or friends, which can lead to fallout if the portrayal is seen as unfavourable or unsympathetic. But there is really no equivalence here. The Aboriginal writer's characters are regarded by their peers as representative of a community: and with so few of them portrayed on stage or screen, they quickly come to be accepted as archetypes. This is a heavy burden for the artist. Gavin Walburgh spoke of Aboriginal filmmaker Rachel Perkins's apprehension regarding the community's response to her 1998 film *Radiance*:

> [She] cannot speak for an entire community, no filmmaker can, yet their reactions to her films remain one of the most important considerations she would no doubt have to grapple with. [...O]ne of the most important things [for her] was the reaction of Aboriginal audiences to her films, believing that they would be 'the biggest critics'.[45]

This is a reflection of the importance attached to storytelling in Aboriginal cultural life. Plays are more than a form of entertainment. While a Western audience might have little quibble with virtually any material, so long as an engaging conflict has been created, an Aboriginal audience tends to view a play dealing with Aboriginal characters as an authentic representation of their community and culture; and insist that it be an appropriate reflection of community values and concerns. The members of the community will 'growl' (scold), or even reject, a writer whom they feel has portrayed Aboriginal life in a way regarded as untruthful, misleading or unacceptable—and this might apply to the depiction of less positive aspects of Aboriginal life. Authenticity is more desirable than conflict but there is pressure not to 'air dirty linen', There could be community backlash, even shunning, if the message is not a positive one—not only for the storytellers, but for the actors. This sensitivity has its roots in the historical way in which we have been portrayed by whitefellas.

This is rarely, if ever, the case for mainstream, non-Aboriginal actors, even when they are portraying a living figure who has questionable morals or values. When I talk about community backlash, I acknowledge, of course, that there is no single community, and no consensus of opinion from an Aboriginal audience/community. As happened with my play *Rainbow's End*, about three generations of Aboriginal women in Victoria, one audience member might disapprove of the way a character is portrayed, and another applaud the portrayal *for exactly the same reasons*. Both, expect that you, the writer, must agree with, and take account of, their viewpoints. You have a responsibility to present a story that matches 'their' story. As an Aboriginal writer I am anxious about how I portray my Aboriginal characters, wanting neither to offend communities nor to feel thwarted. While I acknowledge the strength and resilience of Aboriginal people I know, I also sometimes want to write about situations that are not positive. I want to write what is *real*, and sometimes that's not always nice (or politically correct). But I write, I hope, with empathy and compassion.

Sally Riley, manager of the Indigenous branch of the Australian Film Commission, also speaks of the pressures on Aboriginal filmmakers: what she calls 'a tension between responsibility to your community and responsibility to your craft',[46] words that echo Jack Davis's view that 'writing itself [...] is a political act, a splitting of the mind between one's own thought and the demands of black politics'.[47] Ivan Sen is one Aboriginal filmmaker who is adamant that he doesn't want to be regarded as making 'issues films', and resents the limitations of being pigeon-holed:

> [Sen] described his recent projects as 'stories about me and my family', and has plans for several features to be shot overseas that don't have

> Aboriginal subjects. Young Aboriginal filmmaker Catriona McKenzie is also wary of labels. She has made several award-winning shorts: one of them, *The Third Note*, stars Deborah Mailman. But the important thing about the character she plays is not her Aboriginality, says McKenzie: it's the fact that she's blind.[48]

Another is Richard Frankland, who agrees that the creator can 'become categorized as a message giver as opposed to an entertainer.'[49]

It is Marcia Langton's view that activism is expected, especially of Aboriginal women filmmakers, whose contribution, she asserts,

> lies especially in their distinctive narratives of the familial tensions of their lives, grounded and gendered in their post-colonial Aboriginal identities, their ability to transform Aboriginal traditions, such as the mythological tropes and orality into cinematic forms, in their *duty as cultural activists* and in their exemplary artistic and aesthetic gifts.[50]

Another pressure for the Aboriginal writers is the requirement, that they portray Aboriginal people on page, stage or screen, in a manner that will be educative for a non-Aboriginal audience. As Frances Peters-Little observed in 2004:

> In the protocols and guidelines of the Australia Council, this year the ATSIA board have confirmed that Indigenous […] writers take on the responsibilities of being more than academics and artists, but take on the role of being educators. They are the informants of Indigenous history, art, law and culture.[51]

However laudable the objective of educating non-Aboriginal audiences/readers might be, it can also be burdensome for the dramatist/writer. Since our work will be up for close scrutiny, being educational means being factual, and this alone is an onerous task and not always compatible with the desire to excite and entertain. Is it likely that a non-Aboriginal actor will be able to embody an Aboriginal character in such a way as to be educational? The dramatist faces stern challenges in dealing with Aboriginal themes; how much harder must it be for the performer charged with interpreting their words on the stage or screen?

Although, of course, not identical to those of Aboriginal writers, the anxieties felt by non-Aboriginal writers are also real and, as Germaine Greer has written, have to do with not giving offence:

> White Australians are in the main anxious to avoid upsetting black Australians by referring to them in ways they might find offensive, but at the same time they are so unfamiliar with black people that they have no way of knowing what gives offence and what doesn't.[52]

Consequently, certain areas of exploration constitute dangerous territory for the non-Aboriginal playwright, especially if they are to be dealt with critically. In 2007, for example, Louis Nowra published his non-fiction *Bad Dreaming*, which confronted the subject of Aboriginal male violence. Despite the strong connections that Nowra previously had with members of the Aboriginal community, the book triggered a furious response, especially, but not exclusively, from Aboriginal men, who, not for the first time, felt stereotyped and demonized. One young Aboriginal male, when asked his opinion of the book, said he anticipated it would lead to 'a fresh bout of disapproving stares from people in the street assuming that because he was a black man, he bashed and raped women'.[53]

The opposite approach to Nowra's is the tippy-toeing around Aboriginal 'issues', or the viewing of Aboriginal issues through the lens of 'white guilt'. Guilt can shadow the non-Aboriginal creative trying to incorporate Aboriginal themes, as Rolf de Heer acknowledges in reference to his 2006 *Ten Canoes*, a film depicting Aboriginal life in two distant pasts:

> In the end, it's like there is a lot of guilt involved (in those other films). So I guess where this one fits is that it's the first truly guilt-free one. In its story and subject matter there's nothing that allows us to connect it with white guilt.

Are non-Aboriginal people *allowed* to comment on or be curious about exploring Aboriginal issues? Yes, though in the present climate it is unacceptable, or not politically correct, to *criticize*. Ever since white contact Aboriginal people and culture have been systematically ignored, condescended to and negatively stereotyped. Is it any wonder then that they are ultra-sensitive to criticism, even when it comes from within their own ranks? It follows, therefore, that non-Aboriginal people should approach Aboriginal topics with caution. It is proper that they manifest symptoms of anxiety and doubt around their ability and authority to 'speak' to Aboriginal subjects, no matter how Indig-curious they might be.

5

Can Aboriginality be learnt?

We all can, and should, learn more about Aboriginal history, but can 'Aboriginality' itself be learnt? Greer insists that '[t]here is no "gene" for Aboriginality'. So, if there is no biological difference in cultures, it follows that it is 'nurture' rather than 'nature' that defines a culture. She goes on to declare that 'acquiring Aboriginality is to a large extent the getting of knowledge'.[55] Or, as editor Peter Craven puts it, 'Aboriginality, for her, is not a matter of lines of descent, of genes and blood, it is a getting of wisdom and of understanding.'[56]

Can this be possible? Anecdotally, there are examples of people who have integrated into the Aboriginal community, even to the extent of being initiated. And there are people who have a strong affinity and connection with a community, or who believed they had Aboriginal heritage but discovered they did not; and who are still accepted by some members of their community. For example, Aboriginal activist Gary Foley, argues that writer Mudrooroo (Colin Johnson) has 'earned his stripes', although his identity as an Aboriginal person has been questioned. Foley appears to be in agreement with Greer:

> What the critics of Mudrooroo seem not to appreciate is that to acquire an Aboriginal identity

> (regardless of how) in 1965 was not exactly something that people were queuing up to do […] To have been bestowed with an Aboriginal identity and then embrace and live that identity among Aboriginal people when times were tough is, for me, sufficient for Mudrooroo to be regarded as a member of the Aboriginal community.[57]

Foley is less sympathetic towards Archie Weller, another writer whose Aboriginality has been questioned, even though the latter seems to agree with him that one's acceptance as an Aboriginal person by the community should be factored into the criteria:

> Proving descent should be a 'detail' in deciding who is Aboriginal [...] If you grow up in a West Australian country town and you think you are Aboriginal and people think you are Aboriginal, you bloody well are.[58]

But Foley was not convinced that 'rich kid' Weller *had* been thought of as Aboriginal in his local town. According to Foley, the important distinction was that Mudrooroo lived as an Aboriginal person, his identity was tied to that of being an Aboriginal person. He copped the 'bad' with the 'good'. Once again, my aim here is not to confirm or deny any person's Aboriginality, but to remind us that the issue of our identity is a delicate one. As Mudrooroo poignantly reminds us, 'I had discovered that identity is a fragile thing and can be taken away, just as it can be given.'[59]

Greer states that we should think of Aboriginality 'as a nationality', if it is not from our biology and uses the example of a 'man of Algerian descent who is born in France declaring that he is French; birth and not race is the criterion of nationality'.[60] But isn't it up to this 'man of Algerian descent who is born in France', not Greer, to state how he identifies? Isn't this another example of the dominant 'other' defining our identity? He may think of himself as Algerian, he may think of himself as French or French/Algerian. It might also depend on how others in the community see him; the expectations of others can play a huge part in shaping our identity. I was once asked, after speaking about my 1998 play *Stolen* at a public event, why I referred to myself as 'Aboriginal' and not 'Australian'. My reaction was to ask whether the questioner regarded the terms as mutually exclusive. And in a radio interview, also about *Stolen*, I was asked: 'Do you feel more Aboriginal at the end of this [the playwriting] process?' I was gobsmacked. I felt the interviewer's subtext was that I needed to learn how to be Aboriginal, that somehow I had not been 'fully' Aboriginal before writing *Stolen*.

How does our 'identity' affect the *playing* of an Aboriginal character in a play? A lifelong embeddedness in the Aboriginal community, as is Mudrooroo's experience, might give us the grounding in 'being Aboriginal', even if the biological heritage is absent, but this is hardly the situation of an actor inhabiting a role for a relatively short time. The actor can hardly be expected to absorb, understand, and therefore reflect accurately, the nuances that make up the package we label 'Aboriginality'. For example, could a non-Aboriginal actor 'pull off' the role of an Aboriginal character, albeit a light-skinned Aboriginal, convincingly? Award-winning actor Greg Stone believes it is a measure of the actor's craft, not cultural background, which would make it believable. But the fact that it is possible does not make it *acceptable*.

Aboriginal artistic director Sam Cook believes most non-Aboriginal people do not have the basic cultural understandings to be able to do that kind of role justice:

> I don't think we've gotten to the code of conduct around what the sector tolerates. However, personally I feel that until there's cultural competency and an understanding of Indigenous culture, identity and space, this type of representation would only amount to a caricature and therefore be [...] offensive.

6

Lessons learnt—no longer 'blacking up'

In the—not so distant—past, white actors would 'black up' to play Aboriginal roles in film, TV and theatre. This was inappropriate and downright offensive. The 1967 film *Journey out of Darkness* is

> saddled with a title that betrays the film's view of being Aboriginal. If that wasn't bad enough, white actor Ed Devereaux [...] blacked up for the role of an Aboriginal tracker and Sri Lankan-born singer Kamahl [...] played the role of the Aboriginal killer.[61]

Disturbingly, there are still instances of actors—black actors—being required to 'black up'. For example, only recently, in Baz Luhrmann's *Australia*, Aboriginal actor Ursula Yovich's skin was darkened for her role as the mother of the 'half-caste boy', Nullah.

When Aboriginal people have control over their cultural expression, they often make different kinds of casting decision. *The Cherry Pickers* was first performed with an all-Aboriginal cast in 1971, but not again for more than twenty years, as Kevin Gilbert 'refused to license the piece for production until it could be performed by an all-Aboriginal troupe. This did not occur until a year after his death in 1993.'[62] But Aboriginal people are not always in a position to make those kinds of choices. After searching Australia-wide for eighteen months for a suitable actor for the role of the 'part-Aboriginal' detective in the 1972–3 TV series *Boney*, the producers cast a white New Zealand actor, James Laurenson, in the title role. They needed, as Don Storey put it,

> someone with [the] experience and expertise [to] sustain a sole lead role in a series, and be thoroughly believable as the complex half-caste character—and he had to look the part. The physiognomic requirement immediately excluded many [otherwise competent] actors.'

The producers were fixated on the look of an actor in making their selection:

> James Laurenson said that [producer John] McCallum was being 'frightfully polite and gentlemanly' when they were settling the final details. 'He was saying, "We do think you're

absolutely right for the part with your wide cheekbones and your, ahh, nose is the, umm, right shape, ahh, and your, er, lips ..." and he began to dry up, obviously feeling very embarrassed.

The preference for James Laurenson over an Aboriginal actor angered Aboriginal activists, including the actor and activist Bob Maza. But Laurenson himself, although sympathetic to the feelings of the Aboriginal community, declared that he thought

> an actor has the right to play any part if he believes he can do it, [...] no matter what colour he is. And in that sense I have a right to have a go at playing Boney who is, after all, a half-caste, so as a white I'm half-way there in terms of blood.[63]

The series was remade in 1993 and, unbelievably, another white actor, Cameron Daddo, was cast in the lead. The title was now *Bony* and the character described as a descendant of the original detective. Again, there was protest at the casting, this time with some—limited—success, as the role was adjusted and Bony became 'a white man who once lived with Aboriginals.' But what really happened here was that the producers chose to erase the character's cultural identity rather than cast an Aboriginal actor. So, what progress had been made towards representation on our screens over these 21 years? In a word, little. Where once an Aboriginal protagonist—albeit played by a white man—could be expected to attract a screen audience, it was now no longer acceptable.

Thankfully, the days of white actors playing Aboriginal roles in heavy makeup—which took up to half a day to apply in the case of the first series of *Boney*—are behind us. Unless, that is, we're talking of parody or satire, such as Chris Lilley's 2005 ABC-TV mockumentary *We Can Be Heroes*, in which he created the character of Ricky Wong, a Chinese student who plays an Aboriginal male in his school musical. (Incidentally, Rachael Maza found Lilley's performance 'hilarious'.) However, they are recent enough for Aboriginal people to remember them with disgust. But, the issue of skin-colour aside, how could a non-Aboriginal actor possibly access and convey all of the cultural and political requirements, particularly as many of them are not clearly defined?

It can also be argued that if non-Aboriginal actors are permitted to play Aboriginal roles, no roles will be left for Aboriginal actors. We now have a growing pool of talented and experienced actors, partly thanks to the Western Australian Academy of Performing Arts (WAAPA) and the National Institute of Dramatic Art (NIDA) who have encouraged applications from Indigenous acting students. However these actors are usually cast in roles in which their Aboriginality defines them. Some Aboriginal actors have been able to cross over into mainstream roles, in particular Aaron Pederson, Deborah Mailman and Leah Purcell, and most of their 'colour-blind' roles have been in television. Pederson played a detective and a doctor respectively in the TV mainstream series *Water Rats* (1996-2001) and *MDA* (2002–5) and Mailman had a central role in the series *The Secret Life of Us* (2001–5). She commented at that time on the dearth of opportunities in commercial television for Aboriginal actors:

> [A]t the moment I'm the only actor in an ongoing role. Some people think that there aren't many Aboriginal actors around, and if there are, they're not that good. It's stupid. There's such an incredible pool of talent out there and they're still coming out of drama schools. People just need to take a leap of faith...[64]

A counter argument can also be put that it is the actor's skill that makes a role believable, not their cultural heritage, and that a role should be awarded on merit, not race. Colour-blind casting, the subject of director Lee Lewis's Platform Paper No. 13, proposes that actors from other cultures be given 'white' roles.[65] Aboriginal actors can benefit from this. Indeed, many fine Aboriginal actors have played Shakespeare and other classics, and director Julian Meyrick used mainly Aboriginal actors in his 2009 Melbourne Theatre Company (MTC) production of Pinter's *The Birthday Party*. A theatre audience will quickly accept a cross-racial convention once it is established. Does casting have another dimension—is it satire or parody? Is it making a political or social statement or is it a fantasy or surreal? This sanctions a white actor to play an Indian character (Greg Stone in *Cloud Nine*, MTC, 2003) and a middle-aged man to play a five year old (Geoffrey Rush in *Small Poppies*, Belvoir Street, 2000).

There was a rich history of actors against gender long before Cate Blanchett played Bob Dylan in Todd Haynes's 2007 film *I'm Not There*. Heterosexuals play gays (Sean Penn played Harvey Milk in *Milk*, 2008); gay actors play straight. Actors often play races other than their own: a Chinese friend was cast as a Vietnamese soldier in a TV series some years back. And while these practices may be contentious for some, they hardly make the headlines.

So why should a non-Aboriginal actor in an Aboriginal role be any different?' Lighter-skinned Aboriginal actors often complain that they are discriminated against when they try for Aboriginal roles, because they don't 'read' as Aboriginal. Indeed, the perils of casting by colour—whereby unless an actor is 'black enough' to be read by a white audience as black, they will not be cast as an 'Aborigine'—are outlined in Maryanne Sam's 2002 play *Casting Doubts*. And yet there are esoteric qualities that any Aboriginal actor brings to a role, the sum total of their experience, background, family and community relationships and exposure to aspects of culture including Aboriginal English, body language, knowledge of history. As Wesley Enoch has said:

> Even when an Aboriginal actor has pale skin, you can't de-politicize 'skin'. Aaron Pederson, Debra Mailman, Leah Purcell, although they have played 'mainstream' roles, you can't perceive them as anything but political. They have a righteous position, morally obligated. The politics of skin play a much bigger role here than in the UK, where colour-blind casting is more prevalent. There it comes down to an objective measure of [an actor's] skill. Can they do Shakespeare or can't they? Here we don't have that objective measure of skill to the same degree. It is always a political action to put an Aboriginal actor on stage.

Katharine Brisbane agrees that the Aboriginal actor brings 'another' dimension to their performance, independently of the words they're given to speak:

> A successful production of *Radiance* by Wesley Enoch for the Queensland Theatre Company and Kooemba Jdarra aroused a variety of responses, with some audience members recognizing with applause *aspects of Aboriginal life revealed by actors rather than the text.*[66]

Part of the educative process, then, is to demonstrate to the non-Aboriginal audience that Aboriginality is not simply a question of colour. A black audience doesn't have to be educated in quite the same way, even though the Aboriginality of a character might need to be made explicit. After all, members of their own family/community are often similarly light-skinned. That process needs to extend to the 'real world' where light-skinned people such as myself are still told, 'You don't look Aboriginal', as if that fact alone precluded us from being Aboriginal. So, if a predominantly white audience can be educated to accept the lighter-skinned Aboriginal actor, might they accept a non-Aboriginal actor in an Aboriginal role? What the non-Aboriginal actor cannot possibly bring to the role—and this is the crux of the matter—is something ethereal, intangible, a cultural integrity.

Interestingly, when the Aboriginal actors in Enoch's 2009 production of Dorothy Hewett's *The Man from Mukinupin* doubled to play 'white' roles, one reviewer, while applauding Enoch's direction and commenting on the 'depth of Aboriginal acting talent in the nation', felt obliged to weigh into the colour-blind-casting debate:

> Perhaps the real test of our racial maturity will be when we can conceive of colour-blind acting, and allow "white" actors to again play "black" roles - ultimately it has to cut both ways.

I find this problematic, particularly the 'again'. Earlier examples of white actors playing black were offensive to Aboriginal people. We don't want to go there 'again'. But, in the current climate of heightened awareness, there is little chance of a theatre company thinking, even for a moment, that they might flout the unspoken rule of a non-Aboriginal actor ever 'again' playing an Aboriginal character.

While I believe that some non-Aboriginal people can acquire a familiarity with Aboriginal people and culture that would permit them to be accepted in an Aboriginal community, and while I understand that it is the actor's craft that helps them to inhabit a role—so that *in theory* a highly skilled and sensitive non-Aboriginal person might be able to play an Aboriginal role—casting a non-Aboriginal person would serve no purpose, unless it was deliberately to play on an audience's expectations in order to make a point about race.

7

Why white girls don't Dreamtime...

When I was commissioned to write an 'Indigenous-themed' play for two non-Aboriginal actors, my task was to meet the brief without drifting into performance 'appropriation'. I solved it, I hope, by having each of the characters make the assumption that the other was Aboriginal, and that one believed herself to have Aboriginal heritage—something that was eventually demonstrated to be erroneous. The main theme being explored in the play, *Custody*, was their need to belong, as Australians, particularly in the setting of Alice Springs, and their belief that each was Aboriginal was the most potent way to belong. The audience needs first to accept that Inala believes she has Aboriginal heritage; and that she *could* be, without the actor trying to 'play' an Aboriginal person. The play then takes us on a journey of increasing doubt to the point where she acknowledges her heritage to be Afghani. As the writer, I walked a tightrope—but the actor had greater problems.

The non-Aboriginal community seems mostly blinkered with regard to the Aboriginal experience. White culture dominates to the point where few Australians know much about Aboriginal people beyond what the media spoon-feed them—usually sensational examples of crisis and calamity in Aboriginal communities. The dominant culture here has not incorporated Aboriginal practices, spirituality, language, even foodstuffs, in the way that has happened in New Zealand. As the critic Alison Croggon observed in 2007, Maori culture seems to have infiltrated the New Zealander's daily way of life, Maori words having become part of the standard language of pakehas, or non-Maoris.[67] The same cannot be said of Aboriginal culture, which is barely visible in Australia.

Those who *do* know something about Aboriginal culture might assume that everybody shares in that knowledge, but in my experience 'everybody' doesn't. Regularly asked the same questions—maybe because, as a light-skinned Aboriginal person, I am not seen as 'threatening', or maybe because I move in a variety of social and work circles, not just amongst the 'intelligentsia' who all know, or think they know, 'this stuff'. The academic from South Australia who recently confessed, at a forum on teaching Aboriginal content in the curriculum, that until four years earlier he had known nothing of Aboriginal history, is not at all unusual.[68] Indeed, not all Aboriginal people are 'experts' on all aspects of Aboriginal culture—though it is sometimes assumed that we are—and this may be a direct consequence of colonization and the myriad losses Aboriginal people have suffered since white settlement. Some Aboriginal people are disconnected from their culture for those reasons; many, myself included, are on a lifetime journey of reclamation.

As a researcher I interviewed professionals who work with Aboriginal children in out-of-home care. One of them commented that 'clients will often identify with their Aboriginal heritage, but often in iconic ways—e.g. they will draw the Aboriginal flag—but their connection/knowledge to land and culture is limited. For example, they don't know their mob, or their stories.'[69] Furthermore, very little of this side of our shared history has been taught in schools. If there are Aboriginal people who have limited cultural connection, then there are bound to be many more non-Aboriginal people who are ignorant of Aboriginal culture. Germaine Greer rightly points out that '[m]ost whitefellas cannot differentiate between one Aboriginal group and another. Australian schoolchildren are more likely to be able to name native American peoples than they are Australian.'[70]

The 2002 Tokyo International Festival's production of my play *Stolen* had a Japanese cast and director, while the Australian production, with its Aboriginal actors and director, bookended the festival, an arrangement supported by co-producers Ilbijerri. Yet when at the same time several Australian schools approached Ilbijerri in the hope of mounting a school production with a non-Aboriginal cast, Ilbijerri, with my imprimatur, refused. To paraphrase Ilbijerri's concerns, Aboriginal people must be permitted to tell Aboriginal stories themselves, especially when the subject matter is as sensitive as that of *Stolen*, which deals with the Stolen Generations.

Rachael Maza, who is the current artistic director of Ilbijerri, has recently softened the company's stance, believing that when the aim of a production is educational a non-Aboriginal cast is acceptable: 'It is really important that young people understand [our history]. Then it is not about performance; they may do [the production] horrendously [but they learn].'

In respect of *Stolen*, I still hold the firm view that, if the play is being performed professionally on Aboriginal land (Australia), then it should only be performed by Aboriginal actors. However, if it is being staged elsewhere, in a country where Aboriginal actors are unavailable, then local actors are perhaps acceptable. What is interesting is that on these latter occasions themes emerge that resonate beyond the Australian political context. Wesley Enoch:

> When *Miracles at Cookies Table* premiered in Tokyo, [it] was in the context of a long relationship with [...] director Wada San, who had directed several Aboriginal plays [among them, my own *Stolen*, *Rainbow's End*]. For a Japanese audience, by doing an Aboriginal play, they get to examine their own colonial history through an external eye. I find that amazing, that there are universal themes in an Aboriginal play. Outside of the cultural and political milieu of its own country, the piece has an artistic milieu.

Similarly, for local educational productions that have only non-Aboriginal casts available I have accepted the fact. However, when approached for permission, I do request that the school engage with the local Aboriginal community wherever possible, and invite a local Aboriginal person to act as a cultural consultant. For me, this would gain the benefit of establishing relationships with their local Aboriginal people.

The question of whether it is acceptable to cast a non-Aboriginal actor in an Aboriginal role in Australia is, on the surface, not paradoxical. First, why would you want to? Not when, as Aboriginal actor Leah Purcell says, 'We have our own phenomenal actors around.' It has been suggested that the white middle classes, who make up the bulk of theatre audiences, desire 'cultural authenticity', while the black audience, who attend an Aboriginal play to see their stories told on stage, expect nothing less. Given the availability of experienced Aboriginal actors, there would be, in most cases, no *need* to cast a non-Aboriginal actor. There is no longer—if there ever was—any need to 'do a Boney'.

Why cast a non-Aboriginal person when it is difficult for so many Aboriginal actors to sustain careers in this country? A long-standing 'white-out' on our stages and screens thwarts the ambitions of many 'non-white-looking' actors, I would argue, not only those with Aboriginal heritage. Five years ago a newspaper online blog asked: 'In our culturally diverse city, are our casting processes suitably colourblind?' It elicited the following divergent responses:

- I was a working actor [with Indian heritage] in the UK for 6 years. I was cast in regional and national theatre, television, commercials and film. When I returned to Sydney [...] with a rather healthy CV, I was told by one prospective agent that I would get very little work because I didn't 'look Australian'?
- You're damned if you do and damned if you don't! E.g., if you cast an aborginal [*sic*] person you're accused of tokenism or being overtly PC. If you don't you're accused of bias or failing to reflect diversity in the community.
- Who the hell cares? You've got to cast for the character you're picturing in your mind's eye. Unless you're doing a new Benetton commercial, this point is baseless. What if I felt that Jews

> were not properly represented in [the TV soap] *Home and Away*? Would I be cast on that strength alone? With a society this frightened to offend, probably.[71]

There is a certain ambiguity when an Aboriginal play is produced overseas. While director Kenneth Frankel argued that it was vital the American production of *Bullie's House* have Aboriginal actors, financial costs rarely permit this. At a Malthouse Theatre forum in 2007 director Lee Lewis asked why the plays of American playwright August Wilson were not staged in Australia. She had been told repeatedly that 'there weren't enough black American actors in Australia'. To which she replied that Wilson's plays had been staged in Japan with Japanese casts. Similarly, my own play *Rainbow's End* (2005) was produced in Tokyo with Japanese actors, as was Wesley Enoch's *Miracle at Cookie's Table*, which premiered in Tokyo in 2006, a year before its first production here.

Could Louis Nowra's *Radiance* (1993) be played with a white cast? Perhaps. Indeed, in the opinion of Sylvia Wood, the play is 'primarily a representation of the theme of madness', that 'the characters [...] are superimposed on this theme and [that they] could have been portrayed by white Australians'.[72] But is a production of *The Cherry Pickers* imaginable with a white cast? I doubt it.

It boils down to process. Consultation, collaboration between equal participants, following protocols determined by Aboriginal people and Aboriginal people having control—these are the keys. Stephen Page can encourage a white dancer to mimic his Aboriginal dancers as long as Stephen Page, as an

Aboriginal director, is in control. If that dancer were then to start teaching Aboriginal dancing, or produce his own 'Aboriginal' dance, alarm bells would ring in the community—both black and white communities. If you take Aboriginal people out of the decision-making loop, then the process, and the reaction to the final creative product, is usually compromised. The collaborative process can be accounted a success if there is two-way dialogue and the power base has not been shifted towards the non-Aboriginal.

Aboriginal issues and concerns, culture and ways of being, seeing and doing are part of our 'shared history' and *every one of us* needs to acknowledge that. We all need to re-write our history, to recognize the presence and contribution of Aboriginal people. But the inclusion of Aboriginal themes needs to be done with knowledge, respect and insight—however complex these criteria may be to meet—and acknowledge the rightful ownership of those stories. Leah Purcell:

> If non-Aboriginal people want to work with Aboriginal themes they need to bring opportunities to communities—ownership of stories, copyright and royalties, acknowledgement of the people who contribute. We should be given that power. Just because we tell you a story doesn't mean we're giving it away to you. There needs to be collaboration. It is important that we benefit financially.

Perhaps in this dialogue we also need to consider whether Aboriginal writers should be writing for non-Aboriginal performers? I believe they should. After all, Aboriginal people are often bi-cultural. But that doesn't mean necessarily that they should write Aboriginal characters for non-Aboriginal actors. The writer has a responsibility to the community to tell Aboriginal stories, as there is still so much ignorance and misunderstanding and still such a wide gulf between black and white in this country. Aboriginal actors are an intrinsic part of that story-telling process.

Theatre is about exploring ideas, and if you write safe, then you are not encouraging debate. Germaine Greer's *Whitefella Jump Up* was an attempt to ignite debate about what it is to be an Australian, but after a flurry of reactive comments, the debate petered out and we are little advanced. Perhaps, as Greer concluded, 'The whole Aboriginal question ends up consigned to the too-hard basket, and there we are content to let it stay.'[73]

And yet there is an unmet need from non-Aboriginal people that is encapsulated in the kind of hesitant questions that so many acquaintances have put to me. As one of them, Sandy Garrett, said, 'I would like to know more. I have so many questions.'

In my plays am I helping non-Aboriginal people to 'dance'? First we must rekindle and strengthen our own dances, our own 'web of dreams', but to facilitate that we must also educate non-Aboriginal people as to what and who we are. We must share our history and to that end non-Aboriginal people must have access to Aboriginal themes and extend their curiosity about Aboriginal culture. For me, 'I don't know' is a great place for non-Aboriginal people to start their exploration, as opposed to 'we know best'. In the past there has been too much exploitation: whitefellas exterminating Aboriginal culture—not asking, not learning, not seeing the beauty, the richness, the strengths and wisdom—or pillaging Aboriginal culture, using it for their own gains. We need the Aboriginal story to be told—on the page, on the stage and on the screen—as David Uniapon desired. We need these works to be daring, thought-provoking, meaningful and educational. We need Indig-curious audiences and an Indig-curious readership. No Aboriginal person I know wants to exclude non-Aboriginal people from the mix, or expects to see them excluded, but whether it be in matters of research or writing, Aboriginal people have a set of knowledges that we want to express and don't want to feel like our intellectual property is there for the taking. So, right now, at this point in our history, we need Aboriginal people to be in control of the message and the way in which that message is expressed. As three strong Aboriginal theatre practitioners, Purcell, Maza, and Enoch, respectively, have put it:

- What would have *Rabbit Proof Fence* been like with an Aboriginal director?
- Personally, in 50 years it may be different. You [whitefellas] have had 150 of telling our stories and you can wait another 50 [to perform them] .
- The Germaine Greer view, that today, as an Australian, I am going to wake up, look in the mirror and I'm going to make decisions based on my Aboriginality, my connection—that is a long way off. One day in the future, when our job as storytellers is so successful, that will be possible [...] It is a totally hypothetical future and maybe we'll never get there.

Endnotes

Quotations without a source are extracts from private interviews by the author.

1 See David Unaipon, *Legendary Tales of the Australian Aborigines* (Carlton, Vic.: Melbourne UP, 2001), introduction. This collection of myths and stories were first published under the authorship of William Ramsay Smith in *Myths and Legends of the Australian Aboriginal* (1930). For decades Unaipon received no credit for his scholarship.

2 At http://articles.latimes.com/2010/jan/23/sports/la-spw-skate-dance23-2010jan23 (accessed 12 September 2011).

3 At http://www.associatedcontent.com/article/2728617/olympic_ice_dancing_controversyprotests_pg2.html?cat=9 (accessed 12 September 2011).

4 At http://articles.latimes.com/2010/jan/23/sports/la-spw-skate-dance23-2010jan23 (accessed 12 September 2011).

5 *Whitefella Jump Up: The Shortest Way to Nationhood*, Quarterly Essay 11 (Melbourne: Black Inc., 2003), p.76.

6 *Whitefella Jump Up*, p.39.

7 At http://www.assets.theartscentre.net.au/shortandsweet/rscs/2007%20Files/WRITER_ITC;%20Feedback%20notes.pdf (accessed 16 July 2006).

8 Quoted by Gavin Walburgh, 'Indigenous Representations and Identity in the Films of Rachel Perkins', at http://www.lakemac.infohunt.nsw.gov.au/library/links/hschelp/english/radiance.htm (accessed 26 April 2006).

9 'Writing about Indigenous Australia: Some Issues to Consider and Protocols to Follow: A Discussion Paper', *Southerly*, 62.2 (2002), pp.197–205. at http://www.asauthors.org/lib/pdf/Heiss_Writing_About_Indigenous_Australia.pdf (accessed 30 November 2007).

10 '*Wandering Girl*: Who Defines "Authenticity" in Aboriginal Literature?', in *Blacklines: Contemporary Critical Writing by Indigenous Australians*, ed. By Michele Grossman (Carlton, Vic.: Melbourne UP, 2003, p.182..

11 Speaking at a session of the Tasmanian Readers' and Writers' Festival, September 1998, at http://www.australianhumanitiesreview.org/archive/Issue-September-1998/wright.html (accessed 25 April 2006).
12 *At Allen & Unwin: Notes for Reading Groups: Alex Miller, Journey to the Stone Country*, p.12, at http://www.allenandunwin.com/_uploads/BookPdf/ReadingGroupGuide/9781741141467.pdf (accessed 11 May 2005).
13 *Ibid*, p.10.
14 'An Overview of the Presence of Indigenous Characters in Australian Fiction', text delivered at the University of Granada, December 2001, at http://www.carmelbird.com/indigenous.htm (accessed 26 April 2006).
15 *'Well, I heard it on the radio and I saw it on the television: an essay [...] on the politics and aesthetics of filmmaking by and about Aboriginal people and things* (North Sydney, NSW: AFC, c1993), p.9.
16 'Aborigines, Film and Moffatt's *Night Cries: A Rural Tragedy: An Outsider's Perspective', Bulletin of the Olive Pink Society*, 2.1 (1989), pp.13–7.
17 '*Wandering Girl*: Who Defines "Authenticity" [...]?', pp.181, 187.
18 At http://theatrenotes.blogspot.com/2011/08/review-namatjira-rising-water.html (accessed 11 October 2011).
19 Details of these protocol documents may be found at http://www.austlii.edu.au/au/journals/AILR/1999/51.html (accessed 14 August 2005).
20 On the false claims regarding *Mutant Message Down Under*, see http://www.creativespirits.info/resources/books/mutantmessage.html (accessed 16 April 2009).
21 Marcia Langton, 'Grounded and Gendered: Aboriginal Women in Australian Cinema', in Lisa French (ed.) *Womenvision: Women and the Moving Image in Australia* (Melbourne: Damned Publishing, 2003), p.46.
22 At a forum on 'Writing about Indigenous Issues', held at Mt Waverley Library, Melbourne, on 6 July 2007.

23 'Grounded and Gendered', p.44.
24 '*BeDevil*: Colonial Images, Aboriginal Memories', Span, 37 (December 1993), at http://wwwmcc.murdoch.edu.au/ReadingRoom/litserv/SPAN/37/Laseur.html (accessed 1 December 2007).
25 'Grounded and Gendered', p.46.
26 Matthew Clausen, *Page 8: Teacher's Notes*, Sydney Opera House, at tn_page8.pdf (accessed 16 May 2005).
27 Review: *Blak Inside: 6 Indigenous Plays from Victoria, Network Review of Books*, API (April 2005), at http://www.api-network.com/main/index.php?apply=reviews&webpage (accessed 4 November 2011).
28 '*Wandering Girl*: Who Defines "Authenticity", p.188.
29 Katharine Brisbane, 'The Future in Black and White: Aboriginality in Recent Australian Drama' (1995), at http://www.kooriweb.org/foley/images/history/1970s/blacktheatre/story2.html (accessed 26 April 2006).
30 Marissa McCall, *Deaths in Custody in Australia: 2003 National Deaths in Custody Program (NDICP) Annual Report*, at http://www.aic.gov.au/publications/tbp/tbp012/part2.html (accessed 13 June 2009); Steering Committee for the Review of Government Service Provision, 2007, *Overcoming Indigenous Disadvantage: Key Indicators 2007: Headline Indicators* at http://www.pc.gov.au/oid/headline_indicators (accessed 14 May 2008); Australian Institute of Health and Welfare, *The Health and Welfare of Australia's Aboriginal and Torres Strait Islander Peoples* (2005), at http://www.aihw.gov.au/publications/ihw/hwaatsip05/hwaatsip05.pdf (accessed 16 November 2008).
31 Australian Institute of Health and Welfare, *The Health and Welfare of Australia's Aboriginal and Torres Strait Islander Peoples* (2005), at http://www.aihw.gov.au/publications/ihw/hwaatsip05/hwaatsip05.pdf (accessed 16 November 2008).

32 *Bell's Theorem: Aboriginal Art—It's a White Thing* (November 2002), at http://www.kooriweb.org/foley/resources/art/bellessay.html (accessed 26 April 2006).

33 *Whitefella Jump Up*, p.19.

34 On Carmen's fraud, see Maria Katolander, 'The Unhallowed Art: Literature and Literary Fakes in Australia', *Text*, 4 (October 2005), at http://www.textjournal.com.au/speciss/issue4/takolander.htm (accessed 16 April 2009).

35 'Intellectual Property Rights for Aboriginal People in Australia', Mots Pluriels, 8 (October 1998), at http://www.arts.uwa.edu.au/MotsPluriels/MP898rvdb.html (accessed 6 July 2006).

36 Quoted by Michael Dwyer, '*History Wars, The Musical*', *Age*, 20 October 2006, at http://www.theage.com.au/news/music/history-wars-the-musical/2006/10/19/1160851052066.html?page=fullpage#contentSwap2 (accessed 5 November 2006).

37 National Gallery of Victoria, Gordon Bennett Education Resource, at http://www.ngv.vic.gov.au/gordonbennett/education/intro.html (accessed 6 November 2007).

38 Quoted by Michael Fitzgerald, 'Both Sides Now', *Time*, 23 October, 2006, at http://www.time.com/time/magazine/article/0,9171,1549781,00.html?iid=chix-sphere (accessed 6 November 2007).

39 National Gallery of Australia,'Impossible to Ignore: Imants Tillers' Response to Aboriginal Art', at http://www.nga.gov.au/Exhibition/TILLERS/Default.cfm?MnuID=4&Essay=5 (accessed 17 June 2007).

40 Bangarra website, *Sun Herald* review, 16 April 2006, at http://www.bangarra.com.au/press/reviews.html (accessed 9 July 2007).

41 Quoted by Jennifer Hopper, *J Arts Crew*, 2006, at http://www.theprogram.net.au/featuresSub.asp?id=3436&state=1&category=248 (accessed 9 July 2007).

42 'Controversy Rules', *Koori Mail*, 21 August 2001, p.38, at http://aiatsis.gov.au/koorimail/issues/pdf/283.pdf (accessed 4 November 2011).
43 Quoted by Lorie Boucher, 'Fertile Roots, Arid Soil: Aboriginal Writing's Struggle to Thrive' (2002), at http://www.writersblock.ca/spring2002/interv.htm (accessed 2 December, 2007).
44 Quoted by Esther B. Fein, 'Aboriginal Actors, at Long Wharf, are Adjusting', *New York Times*, 13 May 1985, at http://theater2.nytimes.com/mem/theater/treview.html?res (accessed 26 April 2006).
45 Walburgh, 'Indigenous Representations and Identity in the Films of Rachel Perkins'.
46 Quoted by Philippa Hawker, *Age* review, 19 June 2006, at http://www.kooriweb.org/foley/resources/film/age19jun02.html (accessed 19 June 2006).
47 Brisbane, 'The Future in Black and White'.
48 Hawker, 'Black Magic: Aboriginal Films Take Off', Age, 18 June 2002, at http://www.theage.com.au/articles/2002/06/18/1023864429878.html (accessed 1 May 2006).
49 Quoted by French, 'Short Circuit: Shorts and Australian Women Filmmakers', in *Womenvision*, p.113.
50 'Grounded and Gendered', p.44 [My emphasis].
51 'Applying the Practical to the Unattainable', paper delivered at AIATSIS Conference, November 2004, at http://www.aiatsis.gov.au/aboriginal_studies_press/news (accessed 17 January 2006).
52 *Whitefella Jump Up*, p.45.
53 Margaret Wenham, 'More like a Nightmare', review of *Bad Dreaming*, 6 April 2007, at http://www.news.com.au/couriermail/story/0,23739,21509924-5003424,00.html (accessed 6 November 2007).
54 Jim Schembri, 'De Heer's Shame Revealed', *Age*, 7 July 2006, at http://www.liveshares.com.au/liveshares-articles/2006/7/7/de-heers-shame-revealed (accessed 7 July 2006).

55 *Whitefella Jump Up*, pp.16, 19.
56 *Whitefella Jump Up*, p.v.
57 'Muddy Waters: Archie, Mudrooroo & Aboriginality' (May 1997), Koori History Website at http://www.kooriweb.org/foley/essays/essay_10.html (accessed 17 July 2006).
58 Quoted by Foley.
59 Quoted by Foley.
60 *Whitefella Jump Up*, p.15.
61 Peter Krausz, 'Screening Indigenous Australia: An Overview of Aboriginal Representation on Film', at http://www.enhancetv.com.au/shop/product.php?printable=Y&productid=12668885&cat=255&page=1 (accessed 1 May 2006).
62 Alfred Hickling, *The Cherry Pickers* review, *Guardian*, 16 May 2002, at http://www.guardian.co.uk/stage/2002/may/16/theatre.artsfeatures (accessed 26 April 2006).
63 Don Storey, '*Boney*', Classic Australian Television Website, 2005, at http://www.classicaustraliantv.com/Boney.htm (accessed 21 January 2007).
64 At http://www.mook-e.com/bio/mailman.htm (accessed 13 September 2006).
65 *Cross-racial Casting: Changing the Face of Australian Theatre* (Sydney: Currency House, 2007).
66 'The Future in Black and White' [My emphasis].
67 At a Malthouse Theatre forum, Melbourne, on 15 August 2007.
68 At a La Trobe University forum, Bundoora, on 5 November 2008.
69 M. Bambett and others, 'Not One Size Fits All; Measuring the Social and Emotional Wellbeing of Aboriginal Children' (2007), unpublished paper for La Trobe University, VACCA & Take Two.
70 *Whitefella Jump Up*, p.45.
71 'Is Casting Egalitarian when it Comes to Race?',

Sydney Morning Herald Entertainment blog, posting of 25 October 2006, at http://blogs.smh.com.au/entertainment/archives/the_green_room/006919.html (accessed 26 October 2006).

72 Sylvia Wood, (1998–9), *Representations of Indigenous People in Film and Text* at http://anenglishpage.tripod.com/indigenous.html (accessed 1 May 2006).

73 *Whitefella Jump Up*, p.47.

Readers' Forum

Response to Nicole Canham's *Democracy versus Creativity* (Platform Paper 29)

Dr Sophie Lieberman is Head of Programs at the Historic Houses Trust of New South Wales.

In *Democracy versus Creativity* in Australian Classical Music Nicole Canham provides a timely and insightful reflection on the tension between the attainment of excellence that is at the heart of classical music practice and the expectation of participation inherent in the policy and funding frameworks that support its performance in Australia. As a practitioner in the 'allied' museum sector, her thoughts and reflections on the disconnect between a 'democratic' policy approach and the inherently elitist training that is required in order to participate as a professional in the field have considerable resonance. As Canham suggests, if we want to resolve the tension between 'democracy' and 'creativity' we need to ask ourselves: 'Who is this for?' and make sure that we create work that honestly addresses the needs, interests and creativity of our audience. A brief review of recent experience in the museum sector supports much of Canham's argument: the value of democratising participation, the unique opportunities offered by social media and technology to collaborate with our audiences, and the role of policy in shaping sectoral practice. I offer the following reflections in support of the argument that those of us who work at creating, promoting and funding the Arts be encouraged to take risks and connect with our audiences and their creativity.

Perhaps because, unlike an orchestra or an opera company, museums are founded on a principle of public education, to varying degrees the 'public' has always been the focus of the work of the institution. Since the rise of museology in the 1980s the tradition of edification—a didactic, educational approach to our audiences—has been shifting to one of inclusion, collaboration and 'connection'.[1] This has been accelerated in the past decade by the rise of new technologies and is shifting our understanding of concepts of 'excellence' (curatorial practices) and 'connection' (audience engagement). A key example of this has been the experience of the Powerhouse Museum where in 2006 a commitment was made to allow the general public to tag and curate their collections using their own criteria using OAPC2.[2] The outcomes have informed decisions about what onsite museum visitors experience at the Powerhouse. Even more strikingly it has added new levels of depth to the understanding of the collections and changed the work of curatorial and research staff in the institution (although not always seamlessly). Online audience engagement has given rise to a dynamic body of research and discussion exemplified by the New Media Consortium's annual Horizon Report, Nina Simon's research on the Participatory Museum, Museums and the Web, and MuseumNext.[3] This research has in turn given museum directors the evidence they need to support decisions that privilege audience participation. Where once Web and Programs units were seen as adjunctive to core business, they now sit firmly within the museum structure alongside exhibitions and collections management. For the museum sector excellence is increasingly measured not only by traditional research outputs but also by the involvement of a wide range of audience groups and their satisfaction with their experience.

Democracy versus Creativity rightly recognises the importance of policy in reflecting social values and shaping institutional decision-making processes. Keating's Creative Nation valued excellence in audience experience as access to standards of excellence in the Arts and placed responsibility for engagement squarely at the feet of the performer. The absence of any cultural policy under the Howard Government created a problem for those institutions that set their agendas in part in response to federal funding. In the museum sector the absence of such a framework—the persistence of the 'bums on seats' model—complicated tensions between the museum as research institution and the museum as cultural institution. In seeking to address this, the sector looked overseas. An instructive, though not uncontroversial, model has been the Department of Culture Media and Sport (DCMS) policy framework that provided a decade of clear direction and structural change in the sector in the UK.[4] As the work of Richard Sandell at the University of Leicester has demonstrated, this policy framework required museums to actively value the voices of a variety of different audiences in their work and necessitated the rethinking of institutional structures in order to respond to policy and funding requirements, structural changes that necessarily redistributed resources towards including— connecting with—different audience groups.[5] In Australia, the fact that the museum sector, like the classical music sector, has had limited success in shifting our audience profiles beyond 'university-educated, reasonably well off, fifty plus', can in part be attributed to the absence of a policy framework that required otherwise.[6]

I don't want to overstate the extent to which the museum sector has succeeded in mediating tensions between 'excellence'—curatorial practice—and 'connection'—audience engagement. Nor argue that we have achieved a paradigm shift. Despite the time and effort that has gone into audience engagement in the sector we are a long way off bumper stickers reading 'I love my museum'. What

I have tried to draw out is the value of connecting with audiences and the methodologies and approaches Canham suggests. Taking risks, asking our audiences to participate in our practice, has yielded benefits for the museum sector and there is a vast body of case studies on which leaders in the classical music sector might usefully draw. Similarly I am not arguing that policy is the panacea; rather that is has and can provide important impetus in shifting standards and expectations. Finally, in drawing these comparisons between the museum and classical music sectors I hope I have demonstrated the advantages of widening the thesis presented in *Democracy versus Creativity* and that we in the museum sector will take from Canham's thesis a renewed sense of the value of connecting with our audiences and even, perhaps, of moving beyond 'Who is it for?' to 'What do you value?'

---

[1]An overview of founding issues in museology is available in *The New Museology*, ed. Peter Vergo (London: Reaktion Books Ltd., 1989).

[2]Seb Chan 'Tagging and Searching, Serendipity and Museum Collection databases' paper presented at Museums and the Web 2007, [http://www.archimuse.com/mw2007/papers/chan/chan.html]. There is a wealth of discussion and exploration of the Powerhouse's experience on Chan's blog fresh+new(er) http://www.freshandnew.org/

[3]New Media Consortium Horizon Report, Museum Editions are available online http://www.nmc.org/; Nina Simon's research on Participatory Museum is on her blog Museum2.0 http://museumtwo.blogspot.com/; Museums and the Web Papers are available at the Archives & Museum Informatics website http://www.archimuse.com/conferences/mw.html; and, MuseumNext papers can be accessed online at: http://www.museumnext.org/

[4]A good summary of the debate surrounding this policy framework is available in the Papers and Notes from "From the Markings to the Core? Sackler Conference for Arts Education", March 2010 available at http://www.vam.ac.uk/content/articles/f/from-the-margins-to-the-core-2010-conference/

[5]Richard Sandell, "Social Inclusion, the museum and the dynamics of sectoral change", in *Museum and Society*, 1(1), (2003), pp. 45–62.

[6]Canham p. 3.